In memory of Michael Wilson and Greg Piggot

Melanie Wilson &
•‑fueL present

Autobiographer
by Melanie Wilson

Funded by Arts Council England and a Wellcome Trust Arts Award.
Developed as part of Fuel at the Roundhouse and Jerwood residencies at
Cove Park, which are supported by the Jerwood Charitable Foundation.
Development supported by ARC Stockton on Tees. Developed at MAKE
2010, an artist development programme supported by Absolut Fringe,
Cork Midsummer Festival, Project & Theatre Forum. Rehearsal space in
kind supplied by Shoreditch Town Hall.

Autobiographer is a poem for performance about a woman called Flora. It is a performance woven from the last remembered fragments of the life of a person with dementia. Turned in the mind like precious stones. *Autobiographer* proposes a gently persistent sort of manifesto to an audience, creating a space in which they may meet the event face to face. It seeks to test the distance between us in the hope that we may enjoy each other and that we may speak directly and be challenged, with affection but without complaisance. This meeting between the audience and performance is precious and careful, and through it, the predicament of dementia unfolds. In its own way, *Autobiographer* seeks to draw upon our love for story and narrative and how the processes of dementia prod us away from that defining need, from each other and from ourselves. If there is loss, then there must also be life, no matter how awkwardly shaped. On this we must insist.

Melanie Wilson

Melanie Wilson is a London-based performer, writer and sound artist. She makes performances, installations and sound walks that centre upon the use of sound as a distinct, immersive agency that is powerfully evocative of place linked to state of mind. Her most recent performance *Iris Brunette*, toured nationally and internationally in 2009-11, receiving Best Production award at Dublin Fringe 2009. Melanie's other work includes *every minute, always* (Edinburgh Fringe 2010), *The View From Here* (One on One Festival 2010), *Simple Girl* (UK and international tour, Edinburgh Festival, Dublin Fringe) – nominated for Best Actress and Spirit of the Fringe Award. As a sound artist, Melanie has collaborated with, among others, Subject to_change on *Cupid*; Peter Arnold on his film *Nightspot* and with Coney for *A Small Town Anywhere*. Melanie is co-founder of Patter Theatre Company (2002-06), with whom she co-devised, performed and designed sound for *A Playful Meditation on Magic* and *The Experts* (BAC, Edinburgh Fringe). As a performer/devisor Melanie has worked with Becky Beasley and Chris Sharpe on *13 pieces, 17 feet* (Serpentine Gallery), Chris Goode on *...Sisters* (Gate), Rotozaza on *5am* (UK and international tour), Clod Ensemble on *Red Ladies* and *The Silver Swan* (Edinburgh Fringe), and Boilerhouse on *Drenched* (nominated for Best Actress in a Visiting Company in MEN Theatre Awards 2006). Melanie has also appeared for a limited run in *Tropicana* and *Money* by Shunt in London.

melaniewilson.org.uk

·fueL

Founded in 2004 and led by Louise Blackwell and Kate McGrath, Fuel is a producing organisation working in partnership with some of the most exciting theatre artists in the UK to develop, create and present new work for all.

Fuel is currently producing projects with Will Adamsdale, Clod Ensemble, Inua Ellams, Fevered Sleep, David Rosenberg, Sound&Fury, Uninvited Guests and Melanie Wilson.

Fuel's recent projects include: *The Simple Things in Life* (various artists); *Minsk 2011: A Reply to Kathy Acker* (Belarus Free Theatre, Edinburgh 2011); *Jackson's Way* (Will Adamsdale); *Electric Hotel* (Requardt & Rosenberg); *Kursk* and *Going Dark* (Sound&Fury); *MUST: The Inside Story* (Peggy Shaw and Clod Ensemble); *Love Letters Straight From Your Heart* (Uninvited Guests); *The Forest* and *On Ageing* (Fevered Sleep); *The 14th Tale* and *Black T-Shirt Collection* (Inua Ellams) and *An Anatomie in Four Quarters* (Clod Ensemble).

In partnership with higher education organisations, Fuel runs a rolling internship scheme. For further information on Fuel, our artists, our team and our internships, please visit fueltheatre.com or call +44 (0) 20 7228 6688.

"One of the most exciting and indispensable producing outfits working in British theatre today." *Guardian*

"The maverick producing organisation who are prepared to invest in adventurous artists."
The Herald

Directors **Kate McGrath** & **Louise Blackwell**

Executive Director **Ed Errington**
Producer **Christina Elliot**
Head of Production **Stuart Heyes**
Project Managers **Alice Massey** & **Rosalind Wynn**
Deputy Head of Production **Ian Moore**
Administrator **Natalie Dibsdale**

   JERWOOD CHARITABLE FOUNDATION

Fuel receives National Portfolio funding
from Arts Council England

Autobiographer toured the UK in 2011 and went on to play at Toynbee Studios, London, 17 April – 5 May 2012 and Bristol Old Vic Studio as part of Mayfest 22 – 24 May 2012.

With special thanks to
Catherine Dyson, Sabina Netherclift, Bernadette O'Brien,
Anneke Phillips, Abigail Conway, Chris Thorpe,
Ant Hampton, Jules Deering, Martin Welton and Bridget
Enscolme at Queen Mary University of London
and Battersea Arts Centre.

AUTOBIOGRAPHER

Melanie Wilson

AUTOBIOGRAPHER

OBERON BOOKS
LONDON

WWW.OBERONBOOKS.COM

First published in 2012 by Oberon Books Ltd
521 Caledonian Road, London N7 9RH
Tel: +44 (0) 20 7607 3637 / Fax: +44 (0) 20 7607 3629
e-mail: info@oberonbooks.com
www.oberonbooks.com

A catalogue record for this book is available from the British Library.

PB ISBN: 978-1-84943-482-9
EPUB ISBN: 978-1-84943-610-6

Cover image Melinda Podor. Getty Images.

Printed, bound and converted
by CPI Group (UK) Ltd, Croydon, CR0 4YY.

Visit www.oberonbooks.com to read more about all our books and to buy them. You will also find features, author interviews and news of any author events, and you can sign up for e-newsletters so that you're always first to hear about our new releases.

Characters

FLORA 1
A girl in her late teenage years

FLORA 2
A woman in her mid 30s

FLORA 3
A woman in her early 50s

FLORA 4
A woman in her late 70s

FLORA 5
A girl aged around 8

FLORA v/o
Recorded voiceover –
representing the internal voice

PART ONE

FLORA 2: It's never been my impression from life that things hang together. It's never been apparent to me, from living, that stories get steadily larger.

But rather…that filaments of attachment thread between the most disparate of things…of people… events…words. I've always found that quite… inspiring…reassuring somehow. Ingenious.

And yet now, I get into it, and the things…people… events…words rise up and get me by the nose and all I can do is follow until they stop.

FLORA 3: Here's one…

There is a stone wall against my back, and I'm looking out across a field. I've been there, soaking up his familiar outline for most of the morning. A quietly panicking sponge.

It's biting. November…I think. Which makes me feel worse.

I must have this one still because it was one of those times where what had gone before changed into what went after. A definitive day.

I do remember my father saying, 'Let it out. You must let it out'. I wouldn't. I wouldn't let it out. I'll never let it out. It means something more now. It's something left.

Because sometimes you'll ask. And I really think you'll mean it. You'll say…

FLORA 1: …'How are you feeling?' And I'll think. 18. Inside I feel like I'm 18.

I'm talking to you now before I forget. Here's one…

It's quite cold. I'm wearing mittens. And I'm looking out across the field. He's there in the distance, like he always is.

I feel such a traitor.

I've been up to him already, for a chat. To say hello. With apples. He was really interested. Which made me feel worse. It seems very quiet, but there was wind, so…I'm not sure how that works.

I can't remember how it goes from the field to the gate. How we all got to be there, outside the gate, but then we were there, all of us and none of us speaking, all just focused on him, the member of the family in the frame. It was better to take the rug off she said, so someone did and he stood there all exposed and tucked in the cold wind, very shrunken, which could have been a reason, could have made it logical, but just made it seem more cruel. It seemed cruel.

And then it all sped up, hurtling into one small prick of conclusion, and there was a bit of a panic and not enough time and a little wave of shitting shitting fuck it, this was not how it was meant to be and then I was horizontal on the grass with my cheek on his neck, and feeling like I had a job and feeling like I could do this job really, really well as I had been thinking about it coming for a long time.

More time please

Because sometimes you'll ask…

FLORA 2: ...And I really think you'll mean it. You'll say, 'How are you feeling?' And I'll think...I am an 76-year-old woman, but inside I feel like I'm 33. Just to let you know. Before you forget.

Here's one I know.

Between 30 and 35 degrees latitude, north and south, lie the Horse Latitudes, a subtropical region with little rain and variable winds mixed with calm.

This term, Horse Latitudes originates from a time when ships transported horses to colonies in the west. In this region, these ships would often become becalmed in mid-ocean.

Hours and days pass without breath or thought.

As the drinking water dwindled, so the dead and dying horses were pushed overboard.

Geography A Level. It comes to me now...

FLORA 4: ...very clearly just what I wanted to tell you.

I know this one. The sky is grey. Grey and low. The sky is angered. As if it knows what I'm doing. It seems very quiet...I'm not sure.

It is a kind decision, but that just makes it seem more cruel. It seems cruel. He's cold. Put his blanket back on.

I somehow understand that it is there that I began to be what I am today.

I remember the vermilion in his nostril. On his neck. On my mitten. His familiar outline on the grass. His mane flung out, where he fell. As if flying.

It's something more now: a pause. Where no pause lived before. A small, brittle, restless, turning over. Reflected in someone's glasses.

PART TWO

I.

FLORA 4: It comes to me now, very clearly, just what I wanted to tell you.

FLORA 1: I want...home

FLORA 4: I'd like to go home

FLORA 1: at the other end of the...

FLORA 4: ...telescope

FLORA 1: where I'm also waiting for home.

FLORA 2: I keep myself free

FLORA 3: Light as phenomena

FLORA 2: Indisputable.

FLORA 3: A dandelion clock

FLORA 2: A packed suitcase

FLORA 3: I keep myself free.

FLORA 2: A dandelion clock

FLORA 3: A packed suitcase.

FLORA 2 3: I keep myself free.

FLORA 2: A dandelion clock

FLORA 2 3: A packed suitcase.

FLORA 3: A dandelion clock

FLORA 2: I keep myself free.

FLORA 1: So that when home comes…

FLORA 4: I can leave now, thank you very much

FLORA 1: it was very nice of you to have me,

FLORA 4: but I really should be getting along.

FLORA 1: Upwards, outside of time.

II.

FLORA 2: I'm waiting for my daughter to come along

FLORA 4: My small girl…picks me upwards, from the edge of time

FLORA 2: which might be quite soon.

FLORA 4: My children have orbited me like planets…

FLORA 2: like shadows around noon.

FLORA 4: They're behind me.

FLORA 2: They're still to come.

FLORA 4: My grandchildren swim on my back, through jellyfish, like sea spiders.

FLORA 2: Lucky spiders

FLORA 4: a piece of the sea in their eyes. They're behind me.

FLORA 2: They're still to come.

FLORA 4: My children sit next to me on the piano stool, their small hands shadowing mine through *Eine Kleine Nachtmusik*

FLORA 2: an echo

FLORA 4: and later, their hands grown, they fumble with the zip of my coat in the front seat of the car, whilst the ageless little night, compacted, plays on.

III.

FLORA 2: I am on the back seat of a car. I am folded up. My spine presses into another small spine, a bit further along. I am lying with my eyes open, looking at the roof of the car, at the black rubbery material stretched over maroon ribs.

A while ago there was rushing and flapping but now there is a puzzling silence.

FLORA 3: I sit up and my skin unsticks from the plastic seat. There is a person standing next to the car. It notices my movement and peers in. We peer at each other from both sides of the glass. I wait for it to say something, or for its face to change, but it doesn't and it doesn't move either.

I notice that the window in the front is a little bit open.

FLORA 2: I lie down again in my little patch of the back seat. Some time passes and I hear a microlite in the distance and closer, the small cracks of the roof expanding in the heat. The gluey sweaty feeling behind my folded knees starts to itch.

FLORA 3: I decide to sit up again. I look out of the window. The person is a bit further away now, standing next to the ticket machine. We peer at each other again, from both sides of the glass. I wait for it to say something or for its face to change, but it doesn't and it doesn't move either.

IV.

FLORA 1: In this skin, the sky is ok. The sky is mine.

FLORA 2: A playground. A parent. A birthday party.

FLORA 1: I laugh into its face. I want it in my bones.

FLORA 1 2: I…make…it…devour…me.

FLORA 1: I know it because it's still in there at the other end…

Sfx – footsteps walking into distance.

FLORA 4: *(Action of hand to mouth.)*

FLORA 1: It's not too late yet to still feel the quarrel.

FLORA 2: My hands begin to signal to the future. As if I only just caught hold of myself before I began to unravel.

FLORA 3: I remember my daughter born…thinking… well, there are two of us now. She was as quiet as a mouse…country mouse…

Get up and have a cup of tea.

I sometimes see her when I look over my shoulder…I recognize her hair. My small girl…there should be two of us now. She liked to find feathers. She would take them up and put them in her hair…

Hair. Hare. Her book…a puzzle in the earth…a rabbit. Or Hare?

'Round and round, I follow you, round and round, you follow me.'

Most parents don't know *really*, their children.

Just imagine how it feels.

How would we know?

'Now just imagine how it feels

When first your toes and then your heels,

And then by gradual degrees,

Your shins and ankles, calves and knees,

Are slowly eaten, bit by bit…'

V.

FLORA 4: I am a dress pattern.

FLORA 3: I am the dress pattern of a mother.

FLORA 2: I am the dress pattern. My mother made me.

FLORA 1: The pattern of the dress my mother made.

FLORA 4: She gave me the pieces.

FLORA 1: She put them together for me.

FLORA 2: I picked them apart and made myself differently.

FLORA 3: 'Who does she take after?' someone asks

FLORA 1 2 3 4: Herself

FLORA 1: says my mother

FLORA 1 2 3 4: she takes after herself

FLORA 2: I take off after myself, through the years

FLORA 1: chasing

FLORA 3: chasing

FLORA 4: sewing

FLORA 3: unpicking

FLORA 4: patching

FLORA 1: I've only just put myself together.

FLORA 2: The pattern of me is fraying.

FLORA 4: My pattern is fading, deranging, ageing.

FLORA 3: My girl, my small girl is missing,

FLORA 2: the pattern of me rearranged and when I looked again…

FLORA 3: …there was a space where she stood.

FLORA 1: A space standing proud of other space.

FLORA 3: She is a proud girl, she may not know how to ask for help, she may not be able to ask for help,

FLORA 4: my small girl, missing,

FLORA 1: chasing, chasing,

FLORA 2: rearranging,

FLORA 4: taking off after herself, spilled across the gulf of years.

FLORA 2: A dandelion clock

FLORA 3: A pack of blank space

FLORA 1 2 3 4: *(A breath in together.)*

FLORA 2: …no…not

FLORA 3: A dandelion clock

FLORA 2: A dandelion clock…a pack…

Do you know? *(Asks audience member.)*

(If audience member answers 'a suitcase', then…)

FLORA 2: A suitcase, yes, a suitcase.

(If audience member remains mute, then…)

FLORA 2: Surely it doesn't matter, someone will know.

FLORA 1: It comes to me now, very clearly, just what I wanted to tell you.

FLORA 4: I want…home

FLORA 1: I'd like to go home

FLORA 4: at the other end of the….

FLORA 1: …telescope

FLORA 4: where I'm also waiting for home.

PART THREE

I.

FLORA 3: I have this story…a collection of things…

There was a land of winter.

A land felted with snow.

FLORA 1: A quiet place…

…a wide quiet place of low skies and ebony trees.

Without breath or thought.

FLORA 4: My mother gave me these pieces.

FLORA 3: In a corner of this land

in a small house,

FLORA 2 3: yes

FLORA 2: an out of the way house…

…lived a girl.

Endless winter, with her, a small girl…

FLORA 4: …looking for birds.

Leaving her house, every day…

…into the white wrapped landscape

looking for birds.

Craving their song, their movement, their tiny
industry.

Leaving her house to search for spring as if it were labour.

With…mittens?

FLORA 2: I know this one.

She would bend to the snow…

…to clear the snow from the trunks of trees.

The girl would bend to clear the snow from the trunks of trees.

To expose the earth beneath.

She would bend to ease the icy choke of winter from around their stricken girth.

FLORA 4: To expose the earth beneath.

FLORA 2: I just said that

FLORA 4: Once more…

FLORA 2: I just said that

FLORA 4: …the snow would creep back over the earth to grip the trees once more.

FLORA 3: No sooner had the iron horizon revoked her diminutive form…

FLORA 2: revoked?

FLORA 3: …the snow would creep back over the earth with churlish, patient fingers.

FLORA 1: A small girl in the endless quiet of winter.

FLORA 2: Watched by the other, the opposite… observed at a distance by a boy.

FLORA V/O: An odyssey…

a glimpse of an upturned odyssey…

a ceaseless upturned face…

in search of birds.

They're looking at you

They're waiting

II.

(Performers go to sit with the audience. FLORA 4 chooses a member to speak with.)

FLORA 4: Do you know…what season is it?

(If audience member answers, FLORA repeats their answer carefully. If they remain mute, or demure then FLORA reassures them with…)

[Surely it doesn't matter. Someone will know.]

We've never met before.

I live in London. Sometimes I think I hate the place…so restless…but then it suits me…in my 30s…my insides…I was always a restless, searching sort of person.

Could that make this…logical?

This might sound strange, but it's often the smell that appeals to me. In a thrilling way I mean. The smell of the big city. Perhaps…cooking food on the breeze of a summer evening, blossom, even fumes in an odd sort of way. It's ambidextrous isn't it? Is that what I mean? Well…it's a love-hate thing.

But I do get a lump in my throat about the Marathon. All that sausage of people struggling on, for things they believe in. I'm not talking about the professionals here, the ones at the front.

Or Waterloo Bridge at night…with St Paul's looking like a great cardboard pay gap. Then I bloom…with the thought…I live in London.

There's so much to get done…so much to say, and people even posters telling you the windows are very small, very finite…everyone with an opinion about our bodies. Do you know what I mean? Everyone with an opinion about our bodies. Our imaginations and our dreams outstrip our bodies. One is small whether one feels it or not.

III.

FLORA 1: I have this story.

I was told this story.

Of a boy…a small boy.

And a yearning so profound, that it entered his heart like a clanging bell…

…making it struggle and resist the walls of his chest.

FLORA 3: A small boy…who shaped his heart into a bird

with the sound of the bell

his heart into a bird of green

FLORA 1: brilliant green

FLORA 3: with eyes, shining.

FLORA 1: And a bold beak.

FLORA 3: As the unflinching days passed the boy began to shape his heart into a bird.

FLORA 2: High and bright.

He opened his chest to the air,

and bid his heart fly high and bright,

through the sullen sky to find the girl.

A small girl in the endless quiet of winter.

FLORA 1: I know this one.

FLORA V/O: With her back against a wall

looking out across fields

silenced fields.

FLORA 4: When the bird found her…

she fell to the ground.

He opened his beak and she fell.

He opened his beak and sent beauty into the air,

sending out into the air a tintinnabulation of such outrageous beauty

that the girl fell to the ground horizontal with fear.

FLORA 3: softly now, with the voice of the boy…

FLORA V/O: Little one…spring is coming I promise, but if it doesn't arrive soon I'll go and get it for you myself.

FLORA 2: She heard with ears…ears of her heart.

She raised her face to the future…

in whose plumage, smiling, she caught a glimpse…

Sfx – footsteps approaching from a distance and FLORA 4 puts hand to mouth, then…

FLORA 4: …vertiginously…

FLORA 3: Hmmm…I said it…

FLORA 1: Did my mother give me these pieces?

FLORA 2: I was told this story

Of a boy fetching the spring

I somehow understand it was me.

And it was him…

FLORA 3: A collection of things…that weigh down her head.

The gentle chiming of the bird…that began to recede…

FLORA 2: …as if heard from a great, great distance.

FLORA 4: Every evening, the night hours taught the boy.

Every evening, the bird flew back to sleep in the boy's chest.

He learned of the girl's sadness.

He knew he must go and fetch the spring for her…

FLORA 2: …the other, the other, the echo.

FLORA 1: The echo travelled.

He left with the bird and travelled.

He travelled in desperate search, for nameless ages…

…gone so long like light

FLORA 2: slipped from her mind

FLORA 1: so long gone that the memory of flashing feathers and jubilant soundings

FLORA 3: slipped from her mind

FLORA 4: as if only a passing impression of light through water.

IV.

(Performers sit with audience.)

FLORA 1: I lived in London. With a view behind. From the fourth floor. The windows were very small. Countless aeroplanes in the sky. It was another city up there.

Can you count backwards from 20?

(Asks audience member. They count together quietly as FLORA 3 continues…)

FLORA 3: I remember many small things…sun and breakfast all over the table. There was someone else there…who is it? The face, I don't see it, the sun is behind…I remember the view behind…from the fourth floor…I might have loved this face…I should remember.

Can you spell world backwards?

(Asks audience member. They do it together, gently.)

FLORA 1: It's something different being in the country…town mouse…country mouse…I liked walking…I liked it very much. My legs would take me anywhere. They were very strong. I trusted them, they were my companions. I liked to walk and look at trees. I especially liked trees. Willow trees, oak trees…

V.

FLORA 4: I have this…pattern…to keep hold of

It was me.

It was him.

Where does it go?

FLORA 1: …the base of a tree…

One morning, sitting at the base of a tree,

the truth of the bird.

The blue of the spring sky,

the boy sitting at the base of the tree.

FLORA V/O: 'Little one, I have found the spring and I've brought it back for you'

FLORA 2: The brave eyes of the bird in his

FLORA 3: The blue of the spring sky and the green of the grass in his shining brave eyes

FLORA V/O: 'Spring comes when you return' she said. And the boy replied, the boy replied…

FLORA 4: I will help you remember spring.

FLORA 3: I will help you remember spring. I have seen it.

FLORA 1: I will help you remember spring, that you may have it whenever you need it.

FLORA 2: Let spring live in me and I will carry the promise of it for you.

FLORA V/O: Even if you are alone with winter, the spring will never desert you.

FLORA 4: I could find my way back through it…

FLORA 1 2 3 4: *(All breathe in.)*

FLORA 4: Could I understand?

I might have loved this person…

FLORA 1: I don't want to get married.

FLORA 2: But then…I'm not so sure now…

FLORA 3: Is that because I did?

FLORA 4: And then forgot?

FLORA 1: That's how it seems to me

FLORA 2: You got it wrong?

FLORA 1: I know nothing. I know nothing that's the point

FLORA 3: it's like I know nothing

FLORA 4: I see you…little storm inside me

FLORA 1: fight back. Fight back

FLORA 4: I have this pattern to keep hold of.

(Performers sit with audience.)

VI.

(Music begins.)

FLORA 2: Music makes it alright, doesn't it?

(Asks audience member.)

In this skin the sky is ok, the sky is mine.

I really love my family and I know they really love me.

I've always known it…there's never been any doubt.

I know I'm on my own. We're all on our own…

But they are there…waving from the platform, the car window, the gate, the shore, the bottom of the lane, the top of the hill, across the restaurant, the playing fields, the waiting room, deck chair, an upstairs window, the foyer, the changing rooms, the top of the stairs like the Queen as we wave back,

descending, like the Family von Trapp, laughing.
Loving.

I have to stand up for myself and say what I want…
to let you know…because you will remember and I
will soon forget.

VII.

FLORA 3: What made what just happened be what it
was?

FLORA 2: What happened?

FLORA 4: Once upon a time…

…a very, very bad, quiet place…

…endless winter.

FLORA 1: …with her, a small girl.

FLORA 3 4: Yes

FLORA 3: watched by the other, the echo, the version,
the boy, the small boy.

FLORA 4: A small girl in the endless quiet of winter
watched by the opposite, the small boy. I know this
one.

FLORA 2: More time please…

FLORA 1: Wide surfaces of bad white, huge and wide
and nameless…

FLORA 2: sharp, shattered, silenced trees…

FLORA 3: …the girl gropes, sun remembered days on her fingertips…

FLORA 1: …the saddened boy who watches, who says…

FLORA 4: I'm talking to you now before I forget…

FLORA 2: Spring is coming I promise, but if it doesn't arrive soon I'll go and get it for you myself.

FLORA 1: What a funny thing to say.

FLORA 3: What went after?

FLORA 1: …to recover this one. To go back.

FLORA 4: What made it be what it was?

FLORA 2: Only looking, as days pass like minutes, like minutes passing as hours…

FLORA 1: …until snout of crocus swell of snowdrop.

(In realization:)

FLORA 1 2 3 4: Ahhhh…

FLORA 3: Not spring but something like it…

FLORA 4: some other thing…

FLORA 2: …some stilling, winging in, spreading butter from fingertips to chin.

FLORA 4: I can leave now. It's still in there.

FLORA 1: A puzzle in the earth

FLORA 2: An outline on the grass.

FLORA 3: Yes, I can still do that.

FLORA 2: ummm…I somehow understand that it was a blank place…

FLORA 1: Wait

FLORA 3: No that's not exactly it…

FLORA 4: What a funny thing to say

FLORA 3: Shut up

FLORA 1: I somehow understand that it was very quiet. Quiet…looking…

FLORA 2: For…ummm…for…

FLORA 1: the whole thing

FLORA 4: no that's not it

FLORA 3: Yes

FLORA 2: what happened?

FLORA 3: Quiet…searching…

FLORA 1: You got it wrong?

FLORA 3: winging in…the echo…to recover…

FLORA 1: recover…re…cover…cover…

FLORA 4: or blanket, or sheet, or…quilt?

FLORA 2: What a funny word to use

FLORA 4: Shut up

FLORA 1: Why are you looking at me?

FLORA 4: I somehow understand…

FLORA 2: quiet place, wide surfaces of bad white, huge and wide and…

FLORA 1: I'm sorry?

FLORA 4: …that it was there that I began to become what I am today…

FLORA 3: Black end…blackened…

FLORA 1: Are you listening to me?

FLORA 2: trees…bird…

FLORA 3: to help…little one

FLORA 1: Why do I have this?

FLORA 4: to clear a patch in his heart

FLORA 1: Ahhh..

FLORA 3: something like that anyway

FLORA 2: I'm not sure this is working and also it's quite embarrassing

FLORA 3: dessert

FLORA 4: just so you know

FLORA 2: pudding?

FLORA 4: something like that

FLORA 4: Are you listening to me, I have this thing…

FLORA 2: No one's listening to you anymore.

FLORA 3: What a funny thing to say.

FLORA 1: No, this is about more than all of whatever this is.

FLORA 4: Is this you punishing for not knowing?

FLORA 1: No, this is you saying 'remember?'

FLORA 2: Surely it doesn't matter…someone will know

FLORA 3: Don't look at me. Don't look at me, stop looking at me, stop looking at me, stop looking at me thinking, stop looking at me walking, stop looking at me reading, stop looking at me eating my lunch, stop fucking looking at me, stop putting me in the position of having to ignore you fucking looking at me. Stop spreading your legs so I have to pin mine together.

FLORA 1: It's not me who can't remember, it's you. You who can't remember how incredibly dim and small and boring…how limited and judgmental it begins…how huge and fantastic, how small and dim.

FLORA 4: What am I saying, what am I saying? What am *I* saying?

FLORA 2: Wait…

My breasts don't feel like something I'd do. See…
do you see what I mean? I love you, but I have
absolutely no idea who you are

Quiet…

FLORA 1 2 3 4: quiet

>black

>fuck

>bird

>blue eyes

>fuck

>waiting

Sound and light takes over.

*FLORA 5 walks through the darkened, deafening space,
illuminated in snatches by the ragged flashing lights. She
pauses briefly beside each of the others, touching them gently
on the arm or elbow. As if to test, or to comfort. She leaves
through the door.*

VIII.

*(Each FLORA is located in a quadrant of the space, facing out,
considering the faces of their section of audience.)*

FLORA 1 2 3 4: Ummm…

(Severally and layered.)

FLORA 2 V/O: They're looking at you. They're waiting

FLORA 2: You're waiting for me

FLORA 2 V/O: they want to know…aaah…

FLORA 2: yes?

FLORA 2 V/O: Insert pause.

(Long pause.)

FLORA 2: Nothing more than that?

FLORA 4 V/O: answer

FLORA 4: I'm reflected in someone's glasses

FLORA 4 V/O: answer

FLORA 4: yes?

FLORA 4 V/O: They're waiting for the answer

FLORA 1 V/O: They're waiting for the answer

FLORA 1: All I know is the sound of my voice…

FLORA 1 V/O: Nothing more than that?

FLORA 1: answer

FLORA 1 V/O: Something about…

FLORA 4: yes?

FLORA 3 V/O: They're waiting, watching. They want to know…

FLORA 3: What might happen in these next moments…

FLORA 3 V/O: answer

FLORA 3: I am not here

FLORA 3 V/O: answer

FLORA 3: yes?

FLORA 2 V/O: Someone will tell you the answer.

FLORA 2: answer

FLORA 3 V/O: Someone will tell you the answer

FLORA 3: the answer

FLORA 4 V/O: Someone will tell you the answer

FLORA 4: answer

FLORA 2 V/O: Someone will tell you the answer.

FLORA 2: the answer

FLORA 3 V/O: Someone will tell you the answer

FLORA 3: the answer

FLORA 4 V/O: Someone will tell you the answer

FLORA 4: answer

FLORA 2: answer

FLORA 1: yes?

FLORA 1 V/O: Someone will tell you the answer

FLORA 1: the answer

FLORA 1 V/O: Someone will tell you the answer

FLORA 1: answer

FLORAS turn in and catch sight of each other as hallucinations. They halt abruptly and after a while perform a mirrored gesture together, as if checking the existence of the others.

IX.

FLORA 4: because sometimes, you'll ask…

FLORA 1: There's…

FLORA 3: There's…

FLORA 1 3: a feeling…like

FLORA 1: the sea.

FLORA 3: A strong sea…

FLORA 3: The cold water,

FLORA 1: the situation,

FLORA 1 3: vibrates like a wire.

FLORA 3: The water…

FLORA 1: The water…is

FLORA 1 3: at the top of my thighs.

FLORA 2: A new wave,

FLORA 4: A large wave approaches.

FLORA 2 4: I dive

FLORA 2: into its path

FLORA 4: under.

FLORA 2: It crashes

FLORA 4: it passes above me.

FLORA 2 4: Sleek and pleased.

FLORA 2: It's a fun game.

FLORA 4: I do it again and again.

FLORA 2 4: I turn my feet

FLORA 2: down

FLORA 2: My toes reach

FLORA 4: down and down

FLORA 2 4: in search of sand.

FLORA 4: none

FLORA 2: and now

FLORA 3: another wave comes

FLORA 1: with a lurch.

FLORA 4: Only now that I think of…

FLORA 2: I turn to look for…

FLORA 1 3: the shore.

FLORA 4: Inconceivable…

FLORA 2: far away.

FLORA 1: Up…into the air…on show…useless.

FLORA 3: underneath…further out to sea.

FLORA 2 4: double…act.

PART FOUR

The lighting changes the space in feeling from what has been seen and felt up until this point.

There is an overwhelming auditory environment of real world sounds, like a shopping centre, supermarket or public place. Augmented by fragments of other sounds. Familiar sounds becoming alien.

The performers are engaged in duets of repetitive, restless movement that portrays this atomized, befuddled, crisis state. The movement is partly abstract, but also rooted in gesture and self-awareness. One gives instructions to the other (mostly inaudible to the audience):

> Hand to chest
> Finger to gum
> Hand to face
> The space in front
> Wait

There is a brief moment or two of ranting or raving; of pent-up frustration, from each pair.

The scene ends in an abrupt 'switch off' of both light and sound.

PART FIVE

FLORA 4 V/O: A pattern…moving tree shapes…
beyond the space in front. The temperature…it
seems rolled…matted.

There is someone else here…a low up and down.
More like a pressing in. It moves in time with the
light. What a pleasing trick. I'm sure I've never
noticed this before.

Beyond the space in front is a green part. The green
part is not me…I should check.

FLORA 2 V/O: The light…on my fingertips…it's
happened before. I shall wait and see what comes.

FLORA 3: It's a great city, smeared and buffeted by
paint. I somehow understand that it is here I began
to become what I am today.

FLORA 1 V/O: I do enjoy the feeling of it, warming my
hands. I am here. And he is in the distance. I am
here, a terrible traitor.

[*In what follows, all questions are directed to an audience
member. In each case, if no answer is forthcoming, this line
is used:*

Surely it doesn't matter, someone will know.

If 'I don't know' or similar comes, this line is used:

Nobody around here knows what's going on. I don't
know what's going on either.]

FLORA 4: Where do you live?

(Audience answer: 'I live in X'.*)*

I live in X

I have a daughter

she's very….

What is it? You know…she's…what is it?

(Audience answer: X.)

X, my daughter's very X

FLORA 1: Does this feel like something you would do?

(Audience answer.)

I live in…can you…what is it?

(Audience answer: X.*)*

I live in X

I am a mother

FLORA 3: Do you like animals?

(Audience answer.)

Yes I like animals

I lived in London

I have a daughter

she's very…

What is it? You know…she's good at…what is it?

(Audience answer: X.)

X, my daughter's very X

FLORA 2: What is the weather in your head?

(Audience answer.)

I have a mother

The world is sometimes background, sometimes foreground…

I'm fond of…what do you think?

(Audience answer: X.)

I'm fond of X

Do you know where you're from?

(Audience answer: X.)

FLORA 4: I have a daughter

Have we been here before?

(Audience answer.)

She's from X *(From the previous audience answer.)*

she's very…

What is it? You know…she's…what is it?

(Audience answer: X.)

X, my daughter's very X

I am a grandmother

(Overlapping.)

FLORA 4: can I…

FLORA 3: can I…

FLORA 2: can I…

FLORA 1: can I…

FLORA 4: canulai

FLORA 2: can I…

FLORA 3: ah…

FLORA 1: I

FLORA 2: speaking now

FLORA 4: ah…

FLORA 3: I'm speaking now

FLORA 1: sorry

FLORA 4: speaking these words

FLORA 1: for us

FLORA 3: it all feels a bit…

FLORA 2: horse latitudes

FLORA 1: and yet over here

FLORA 4: vermilion

FLORA 3: as if…flying

FLORA 2: dead horse eye

FLORA 1: in mid flap

FLORA 4: mane spilt over grass

FLORA 3: as if…frying

FLORA 2: where he fell

FLORA 4: vermilion in his nostril

FLORA 3: on his neck…k…k…

FLORA 1: on my mitten

FLORA 3: neck

FLORA 2: nostril

FLORA 1: mitten

FLORA 4: I'm sure I've never spoken of this before

FLORA 3: sorry

FLORA 1: a…space…rocket…exloading

FLORA 2: their families watching

FLORA 1: 20, 19, 18, 17, 16, 15…

FLORA 3: in two, in three, in infinity

FLORA 4: in mid flap

FLORA 1: very fast falling away from home

FLORA 2: landing…in a horse latitude

FLORA 3: Very far away, in the distance, in the life jacket,

FLORA 4: but I can still hear

FLORA 2: just what I wanted to tell you about

FLORA 1: I am still here

FLORA 2: I am still here

FLORA 3: I am still here

FLORA 4: I am still here

WWW.OBERONBOOKS.COM